The Singing Princess

Judy Waite

Illustrated by Nick Schon

Chapter 1

Princess Melody loved to sing. "Singing is my whole life," she would say.

That is why her servants were too afraid to tell her the truth. Princess Melody was the worst singer in the world. Her high notes sounded like cats wailing. Her low notes sounded like cows burping.

All of Princess Melody's servants wore earplugs, so they couldn't hear the princess singing. They wore such big earplugs that they couldn't hear *anybody*. So nobody spoke to anyone else, and life at the palace was dull.

Until . . .

. . . one day, Prince Dance-a-Lot came riding through the land. He heard a dreadful screeching from behind the palace walls.

"It sounds like a terrible monster!" he cried.

The dreadful screeching grew louder and **louder** and **LOUDER!**

Now, Prince Dance-a-Lot had never been much of a hero in his own land. Some people even said that he still took his teddy bear to bed with him.

This was his big chance to be a hero!

He took a deep breath and leaped over the
palace wall. He landed with a crash in the
palace garden. Then he saw the princess.

CRASH!

Princess Melody stopped right in the
middle of her highest note ever. She glared
at the prince.

"Don't be scared!" Prince Dance-a-Lot cried.
"I have come to save you!" The prince waved
his sword in the air.

"Save me from what?" asked the princess.

"The terrible monster! I heard it screeching."

Princess Melody had been busy singing. She hadn't heard any terrible monsters. But she helped Prince Dance-a-Lot look for a monster, just in case. They peered and poked between bushes and trees.

"I think it's gone," said the prince at last.

"You must have scared it away," the princess said. She smiled. "You look a little pale. Why don't you come in and have some cake?"

The servants were very excited. Princess
Melody had never invited a prince to
visit before.

The prince and princess chatted happily.
They swapped stories about frogs and peas
and ugly sisters.

Until . . .

. . . Princess Melody asked, "Do you like singing?"

Prince Dance-a-Lot nodded. "And dancing," he told her. Then suddenly he looked sad. "But no one ever wants to dance with me."

"I know!" said Princess Melody. "I'll sing, and you dance. Then we'll both be happy."

Her servants ran up to her and begged her to change her mind. But they were too late.

11

Chapter 2

Princess Melody began to sing. Prince
Dance-a-Lot began to dance.
Everyone else ran away. It
was an awful moment. The prince
realized there had been no terrible
monster in the garden.

SCREECH!

And the princess realized why no one would ever dance with Prince Dance-a-Lot – he was dreadful! He bumped into tables. He bounced into walls. He even trod on his own toes.

STOP!

"**STOP!**" shouted the princess.

"**STOP!**" shouted the prince.

"You dance like a three-legged hippopotamus on roller skates!" cried Princess Melody.

"And you sing like a trumpeting elephant with toothache!" cried Prince Dance-a-Lot.

They both glared at each other.

Until . . .

. . . suddenly, Princess Melody began laughing.
She had a spluttery, sparkly sort of laugh.
The sort of laugh that made her face go
pink. The sort of laugh that made her eyes
shine like happy stars.

Prince Dance-a-Lot was still angry.
He looked away. He made his face into a
grumpy shape. But slowly a bumbly, rumbly
noise began to wobble inside him.

The bumbly, rumbly noise got bigger
and bigger.

Until . . .

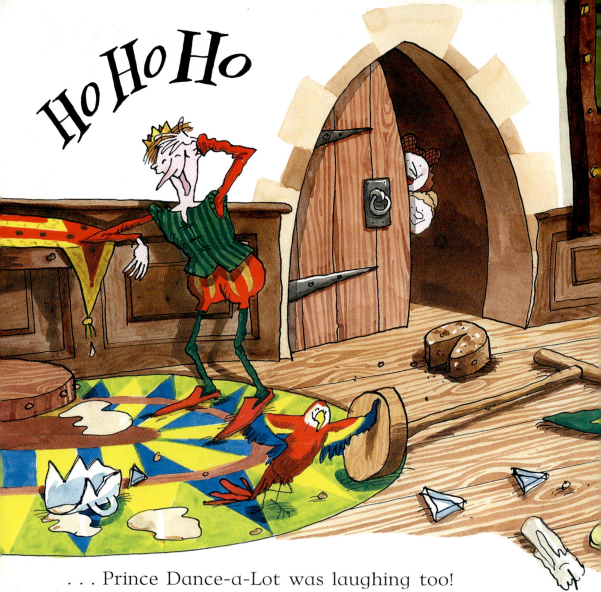

. . . Prince Dance-a-Lot was laughing too!
Prince Dance-a-Lot had a booming,
bouncing sort of laugh. The sort of laugh
that buzzes through all your fingers and
toes. The sort of laugh that makes you want
to hug the whole world.

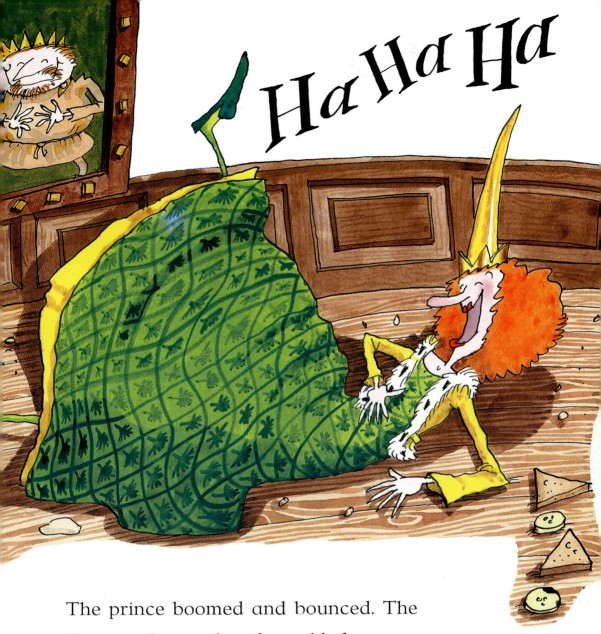

The prince boomed and bounced. The princess spluttered and sparkled.

Then the princess boomed and bounced and the prince spluttered and sparkled.

Until . . .

. . . slowly the servants crept back in. They
started to smile. They started to snigger.
The servants began to splutter and sparkle.
The servants began to boom and bounce.

Soon the whole palace was booming and
sparkling and bouncing and spluttering.

Until . . .

. . . "How long have you been singing those dreadful songs?" asked the prince.

"All my life," said the princess. "How long have you been doing those dreadful dances?"

"All my life," said the prince.

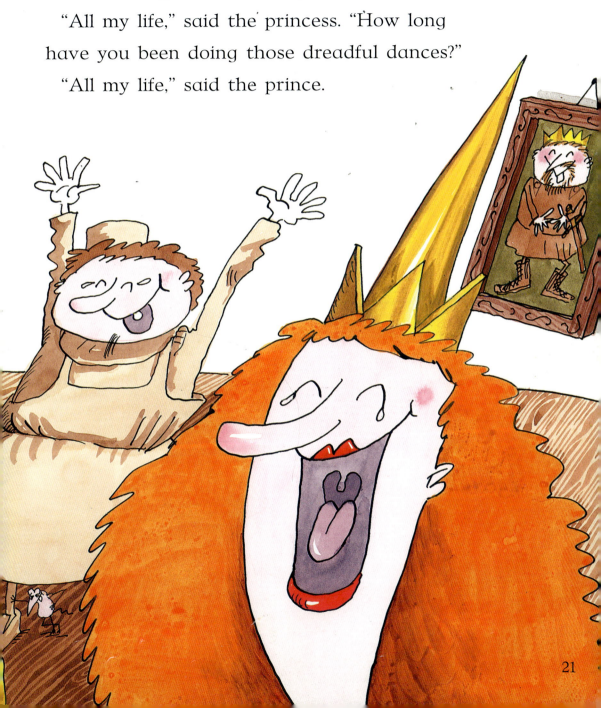

Princess Melody looked sad. "I've been making a king-size fool of myself," she said. "And you've been the only person brave enough to tell me."

Prince Dance-a-Lot blushed brighter than tomato ketchup. "I've been making a regular palace clown of myself," he said. "And *you've* been the only person brave enough to tell *me*."

"We must be made for each other," the princess said. "I think you should marry me."

"As long as you promise never to sing again," said the prince.

"And as long as you promise to give up dancing," said the princess.

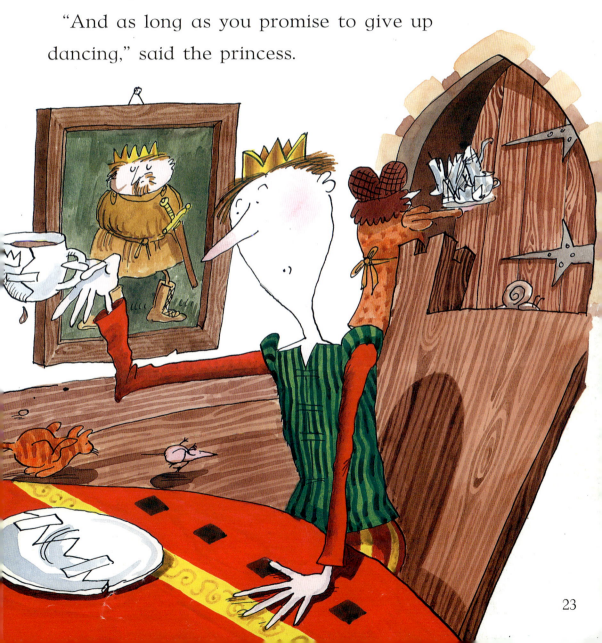

The prince and princess were married,
and they both lived happily ever after.
Until . . .

. . . Prince Dance-a-Lot took up roller skating,
and Princess Melody got a trumpet for her
birthday.